end

In *Unhurried Grace for a Mom's Heart*, Durenda Wilson offers a fresh and encouraging word for any homeschooling mom---whether veteran or just starting out. These 31 devotionals are short, highly doable, and contain a much-needed biblical message for those of us on this often challenging journey. Thank you Durenda for sharing your wisdom and experience to help us along the way!

—**Lisa Jacobson, Club31Women.com**

Durenda's voice is one that is truly needed among the noisy world we live in. Her calming and gentle spirit in her words point back to the ONE voice we should all be listening to- God's. In a time when moms are bombarded with information, Durenda humbly reminds us all to seek the One truth we can depend on. I am confident this generation of mothers will be blessed by this much needed devotional. Stop listening to all the noise, and simply sit at His feet and listen. Thank you, Durenda for this invaluable resource.

—**Karen DeBeus, Author of *Called Home* and**
***Simply Homeschool*, simplylivingforhim.com**

Unhurried Grace for a Mom's Heart offers moms fresh, daily doses of truth and grace for the common challenges they face while mothering and homeschooling. Whether a mom has just welcomed a newborn into the world or has walked through years of experience and needs refreshment, Durenda meets moms where they are on the journey.

—**Cheryl Bastian, cherylbastian.com**

Durenda Wilson has given homeschool moms a beautiful gift in *Unhurried Grace*, a devotional that is refreshingly practical and soundly biblical. With short but compelling readings, paired with passages of scripture and places for journaling, you can take your time working your way through the 31 easy to read chapters. But each one will be a big dose of encouragement, with tried and true wisdom from an "older woman" who has homeschooled eight children. She's been there, done that--with grace. And I, for one, am grateful that she's taken the time to share her perspective with the next generation of homeschool moms.

—Gretchen Louise, founder of Kindred Grace

UNHURRIED

grace

UNHURRIED
grace
FOR A
MOM'S HEART

31 Days in God's Word

DURENDA WILSON

Unhurried Grace for a Mom's Heart:
31 Days in God's Word

© Copyright 2018 Durenda Wilson

ISBN: 978-1983403965 (print)

Publishing and Design Services
MartinPublishingServices.com

Editor
Lauren Stinton

Printed in the United States of America.

For additional encouragement, visit

DurendaWilson.com

dedication

This book is dedicated to you, Moms. That you are holding it in your hands gives testimony to your heart for the Lord and your desire to grow in the wisdom and knowledge of Him through His Word. Your children are blessed to have you. May God be the One who defines you, not others and not the culture around you. Take the time to listen to what He is speaking to your heart, and walk in obedience to His quiet voice. I guarantee that He will be faithful to bless you more than you could ask or imagine, according to His power at work in you.

acknowledgements

My husband, Darryl

Your encouragement and support are an integral part of book writing for me. When you've been married for almost three decades, you get to know each other inside and out, which often ends up being messy and beautiful at the same time. Love doesn't rush past the hard places, but it also knows when to move forward. Loving someone well takes time,thought and prayer. You've given all of these. I'm so thankful, and I can't imagine life without you. Oh, and I really like your muscles, too.

Our married daughters, Brittney and Jenna

You are grown now, with children of your own, and I love our conversations about many things—but especially when we talk about motherhood. I always walk away feeling so thankful for both of you. You continue to amaze me with the insights and wisdom you have at such young ages. Your children are blessed to have you. I am blessed—not only to call you my daughters but also my friends.

Publishing a book requires so much more than I could possibly do on my own. Thankfully I am surrounded by a team of women who love the Lord and who have brought their valuable gifts and experience to this project:

My editor, Lauren Stinton

I love how you totally "get" me and have an uncanny ability to bring clarity to my "voice" through the written word. Your humor keeps me sane through this writing process!

My marketing team at Vividly Social

Trish Corlew

God has used you to inspire me countless times. Your knowledge, experience, and discernment have been such an encouragement to me. I'm so grateful God brought you into this season of my life!

Rachel Lance

During a very busy season of motherhood in your own life, you have graciously invested time into this project. More than that, you have engaged your heart and given invaluable direction at key moments along the way. I am so grateful.

My book designer, Melinda Martin

I don't know how you do it, but somehow you are able to pinpoint the look, design, font, etc. to fit my projects perfectly the first time around! You are truly gifted and such a joy to work with.

Pastor Griff

In a busy, multi-generational household, it can be challenging to find a quiet room to write in. You graciously offered just such a place at our church across the street, and I couldn't be more thankful! God has used you more than you know to bless our family and inspire this writing mom.

Contents

Dear Moms 1
1. Strength in Weakness 5
2. New or Better? 9
3. One Voice 13
4. Loaves and Fishes for Moms 17
5. Jesus' Power at Work in Us 21
6. God's Wisdom or Man's? 25
7. My Ways or His? 29
8. The Heart of Homeschooling 33
9. Redeemer of Messes 37
10. Don't Go Back to Egypt 41
11. Dealing with Limitations 45
12. Working from a Place of Rest 49
13. The Only Opinion that Matters 53
14. Cross Centered 57
15. Wholehearted Trust 61
16. Power Over Fear 65
17. He is Good 69
18. Freedom from People Pleasing 73
19. Wait Patiently for Him 77
20. Mom Care 81
21. Building Altars 85
22. Loneliness 89
23. Contentment 93
24. Shining like Stars 97
25. If Not, He is Still Good 101
26. Wisdom for Everything 105
27. No Worries 109
28. Looking like Fools 113
29. Finding Meaning in the Mundane 117
30. Redemption in Motherhood 121
31. Unhurried Grace 125
Conclusion 129
About the Author 130

dear moms,

This devotional came about quite unexpectedly. I started a podcast with the simple intention of sharing from each chapter of my book, *The Unhurried Homeschooler*. However, as I began to write out my notes for each podcast, God would clearly lay His Word and an application on my heart concerning moms—especially homeschooling moms. I thought it was a fluke with the first one or two, but it continued steadily, and I realized He just might want me to bring a word from Him to moms.

My husband and I have eight kids, and we've been parents for twenty-seven years. I've always stayed at home, and we homeschooled our children from the beginning. Along the way I often wondered if I should be doing something else in addition to motherhood, like some kind of ministry, but every time I prayed about it, God would whisper, "Keep your hand to the plow." There was peace in that simple answer. Isn't it just like God to lift those self-made burdens and give us a yoke that is perfectly fitted for us?

I love this passage in Matthew 11:28–30 (MSG):

> Are you tired? Worn out? Burned out on religion? Come to Me. Get away with Me and you'll recover your life. I'll show you how to take a real rest. Walk with Me and work with Me—watch how I do it. Learn the unforced rhythms of grace. I won't lay anything heavy or ill-fitting on you. Keep company with Me and you'll learn to live freely and lightly.

The blessings of life can feel a lot like burdens. Homeschooling, parenting, marriage, relationships—all these things bring with them their share of disappointments, frustrations, and trials, but God always has something good planned for us. We know this because of Romans 8:28: "And we know that God causes everything to work together for the good of those who love God and are called according to His purpose for them."

Sometimes God asks us to bear hard things, but He never leaves us without His grace. He gives us exactly what we need, so we can do what He asked. Sometimes, however, we can find ourselves involved in groups, programs, and other activities He *hasn't* called us to do, and these "other things" weigh us down, because we don't have access to the divine grace and energy we need to accomplish them. Therefore, it is imperative we slow down and listen for His still, small voice telling us what we should do and the way we should go.

Being a mom, especially a homeschooling mom, makes me think of the explorers of old. Those brave souls forged uncharted territory and drew their maps as they went. Over the years, God has faithfully walked with me, discipling me and helping me through the unfamiliar and often uncomfortable parts of life and homeschooling. He has shown me how to "draw the map" for our family and continues to do so to this day. He wants to do the same for you, revealing His truth, love, faithfulness, and unending mercies that are new every morning. He loves you without end and has done everything necessary in the finished work of the cross so you can experience His redemption daily.

But this isn't something that works without Him. We need to take the time to slow our hearts, seek His face, and listen for His tender voice. His voice isn't still and small because He wants to make things hard for us. It's still and small so when we *want* to hear, we have to engage all our senses. This prepares our hearts more fully for what He wants to say and helps us walk in obedience.

I've often found myself looking for a specific kind of devotional to help me as I charted new territory with my family. The criteria were always the same: The devotional needed to be straightforward and not verbose. (As moms, we deal with *way* too many words every day as it is!) I wanted a passage of Scripture to read as opposed to just a verse or two, because context is important. I wanted to grow in my understanding of God, His Word, and what He had for me in full-time motherhood and homeschooling. I needed to go deeper than skimming the surface, yet I didn't have the time or emotional and mental energy for a full-blown Bible study. Though those studies definitely have their time and place, moms are *busy*. We can't just drop everything and walk away from our houses and families. In my search for the devotional I wanted, I discovered that most didn't offer what I was looking for.

My hope and prayer are that this little book will be for you what I wanted a devotional to be for me. Hear with your heart the words written here—the Scriptures most of all. Everything we need to live godly lives can be found in His Word. It is living and active, and it *always* produces fruit (Hebrews 4:12–13; Isaiah 55:11). The words of Scripture are breathed out by God Himself (2 Timothy 3:16–17). They are sure, timeless, unchanging . . . just like our God. His words are the anchor for our souls, giving us the discernment and wisdom we need to keep from being deceived, help us gain victory, and show us what God has in store for our families.

Get out your Bible and find at least the main passage (in bold type) in each devotion for yourself. Engaging all our senses helps us remember what we've read.

Each devotion gives you two places to respond. You can write out the words of your own heart in prayer, as well as make note of what you are sensing God speak to you. Don't rush past any parts that may seem hard. Breathe deeply and slow your pace to match that of Jesus. Invite the Holy Spirit to work in your heart. If you need to leave the response blank for now, that's okay. You are learning to wait on the Lord. This book contains thirty-one devotions, which you can revisit as often as you like through the year.

Moms, we are in the middle of spiritual warfare every single day (1 Peter 5:8). We have to stay alert, asking God to give us His eyes and ears and to equip us, so we will walk in victory. Our war is not of this world, as 2 Corinthians 10:3–5 tells us, and we have the privilege each day to walk out our faith in our homes and with our families.

What we are doing at home is of utmost importance. We must not let the enemy distract us from our high calling. As mission-minded moms, we understand the threat we pose to the enemy's kingdom, and we stand firm in the truth of God's Word. We don't let culture or the voices of condemnation influence our decisions. Instead, we stay the course, setting our faces like flint.

Because the Sovereign Lord helps me,
I will not be disgraced.
Therefore have I set my face like flint,
and I know I will not be put to shame.

— Isaiah 50:7 (NIV)

—durenda

1

strength in weakness

Read 2 Corinthians 12:5–10.

As moms, it's easy to start feeling inadequate. We wage war daily with the thought that we aren't enough, that we aren't doing everything we should be doing. The pressure is enough to make a grown woman cry and often has—myself included. The enemy uses this sense of failure to get a foothold in our minds and hearts and rob us of God's blessings, both in motherhood and homeschooling.

What is the answer? We need to ask God to help us recognize the lie for what it is.

The most effective deceptions have an element of truth to them. The idea that we are not enough and aren't doing enough actually has some truth to it, which is why the enemy uses it so often and why the lie works against us so well. Here's what I mean:

1. If we believe we can be perfect (that we can do and be enough), we are basically saying we're able to be God. He is the only One who can pull that off. There is only one Perfect One, and we are not Him.

2. If we believe our kids will turn out okay if we are enough, where is God in that equation? Does this mean He blesses us *only* if we've taken care of every jot and tittle first?

Obviously, we have responsibilities as moms. We have a long list of things we have to oversee and complete on a daily basis, but more than anything, God wants us to experience His grace each day at home with our families. He wants us to see Him working and then work *with* Him. He wants us to experience His power moving through our weaknesses. Instead of complaining and bemoaning our weaknesses, we can allow God's strength to show through them.

In 2 Corinthians Paul talked about how God allowed something painful in his life to help him walk in humility. Paul begged God to take it away and referred to this thing as a "thorn" in his flesh. But through it he learned how big God really is:

> Three different times I begged the Lord to take it away. Each time He said, "My grace is all you need. My power works best in weakness." So now I am glad to boast about my weaknesses, so that the power of Christ can work through me. That's why I take pleasure in my weaknesses, and in the insults, hardships, persecutions, and troubles that I suffer for Christ. For when I am weak, then I am strong.
>
> — 2 Corinthians 12:8–10

We shut the mouth of the enemy as we embrace God's truth. In our weaknesses God can reveal Himself in powerful ways.

what god is saying to my heart

_____

_____

_____

_____

_____

what my heart is saying to god

_____

_____

_____

_____

_____

Dig Deeper: In which areas of motherhood and homeschooling do you feel inadequate? Can you see any ways that God may be using your weakness to show His power? Which areas do you need to bring before Him and ask for His strength?

2

new or better?

I f something is new, it's tempting to think it must be better. But Ecclesiastes 1:9 tells us, "History merely repeats itself. It has all been done before. Nothing under the sun is truly new."

It is human nature to recoil against tradition and boundaries. Some of them need to be questioned, while others should be done away with, but certain boundaries are vital for our health. God explains this concept in Jeremiah 6:16:

> This is what the Lord says:
> "Stop at the crossroads and look around.
> Ask for the old, godly way, and walk in it.
> Travel its path, and you will find rest for your souls.
> But you reply, 'No, that's not the road we want!'"

When God created us, He placed boundaries on our lives—boundaries that are good. They are in our best interest. He isn't trying to shortchange us; He is a God of blessing and provision. He is a healer and our Redeemer.

When God spoke to the prophet Jeremiah about the people's rebellion and idol worship, He asked, "Am I the one they are hurting? Most of all, they hurt themselves to their own shame" (see Jeremiah 7:19). God wants the very best for us. Sometimes His very best is discipline and sometimes it's comfort. Often we associate the word *discipline* with punishment, but this isn't the case here because Jesus took our punishment when He died on the cross. God's discipline is more like training *through* hardship, similar to boot camp.

James 1:2–4 (NIV) tells us to rejoice when we face hardship:

> Consider it pure joy, my brothers and sisters, whenever you face trials of many kinds, because you know that the testing of your faith produces perseverance. Let perseverance finish its work so that you may be mature and complete, not lacking anything.

God uses discipline to strengthen and prepare us to have victory over life's battles. No matter how His very best comes, all of it is good, and He gives us wisdom and direction through His ancient yet relevant Word. "Ask for the old, godly way, and walk in it."

what god is saying to my heart

_____

_____

_____

_____

_____

what my heart is saying to god

_____

_____

_____

_____

_____

Dig Deeper: Are you taking the time to listen to that still, small voice today? Do you desire to follow His gentle correction, comfort, and provision? Where in your life has He placed clear boundaries?

3

one voice

Read 1 Kings 19:9–13.

Several times over the years, I have doubted myself as a mom. I would see other moms involved in "extracurricular" things like ministry, activities at church, leading Bible studies, etc., and I would wonder if I should be doing some or all those things.

But how could I? I was overwhelmed just at the thought of trying to do anything more than be a good mom to several children. Yet I still had this nagging sense that I might be missing out on something important.

As I tried to figure this out, I decided the best thing I could do was inquire of the Lord. I knew He saw the big picture, and if He wanted me to be part of something else, He would give me the direction and grace to do so. I asked Him, "Lord, is there anything else that I should be doing other than what I have right here in front of me at home?"

Immediately, I heard His still, small voice whisper to me to keep doing what I was doing. Relief and a strong sense of peace filled my soul. I realized God was telling me that what I was doing was enough, and He wasn't about to put any burdens on me that were ill fitting. The yoke He used was custom made for me, and I needed to be faithful to bear that yoke—nothing more than that yoke and nothing less.

On a daily basis, so many voices call out to us. Many of those voices are good ones, worthy of our attention. But often they are loud and demanding so we need to listen for the most important voice of all—the quiet voice of the Holy Spirit.

In 1 Kings 19:11–13 God wanted to speak to Elijah:

"Go out and stand before Me on the mountain," the Lord told him. And as Elijah stood there, the Lord passed by, and a mighty windstorm hit the mountain. It was such a terrible blast that the rocks were torn loose, but the Lord was not in the wind. After the wind there was an earthquake, but the Lord was not in the earthquake. And after the earthquake there was a fire, but the Lord was not in the fire. And after the fire there was the sound of a gentle whisper. When Elijah heard it, he wrapped his face in his cloak and went out and stood at the entrance of the cave.

To hear God speak to us, we need to slow our hearts and hush the other voices that demand our attention. We wait patiently on the Lord alone, like Elijah did on the mountain.

Remember, there is only one voice we are responsible to listen to and obey, only one we yield every part of our lives to. Only one voice deserves our utmost attention.

what god is saying to my heart

_____

_____

_____

_____

_____

what my heart is saying to god

_____

_____

_____

_____

_____

Dig Deeper: Take some time to be still before the Lord. What is He whispering to you today?

4

loaves and fishes for moms

Read Matthew 14:13–21.

Matthew 14 is one of my favorite passages because in so many ways it reminds me of motherhood. Jesus had just found out that John the Baptist, a family member and a friend, was executed. Feeling the sting of loss, Jesus was in serious need of solitude—but that clearly was not in the cards for Him.

As a mom, can you relate?

I can't tell you how often I have *needed* time to myself, but it usually was at the very moment when alone time was not a possibility. When my children pounded on the door, was God cheating me? When someone started screaming in another room, was God being merciless and ungracious? At the time, my emotions would have said, "Yes!" But my heart knows that isn't who God is.

Though Jesus wanted alone time, the Father had other (and better) plans for Him, ones that involved showing His glory in a real, practical, and extraordinary way.

As Jesus attempted to leave, the crowds heard where He was headed and followed Him (kind of like kids following you to the bathroom). Instead of running for His life, the Bible says, "He had compassion on them." He continued to minister to them throughout the day.

By evening everyone was getting hungry, and He told His disciples to feed them. The disciples replied, "But we have only five loaves and two fish!" Jesus took what little the disciples had to offer, looked up toward Heaven, and blessed the food. He believed His Father could—and would—make it enough. Not only did God make it enough, but there was a copious amount of leftovers!

As moms, we can be painfully aware of our inadequacies, and the enemy delights in shoving them in our faces as he fills our ears with words of condemnation. But the truth is that God is so much bigger than the enemy's accusations! He delights in showing Himself mighty over and over again.

We can take these things that seem like meager offerings, lift them up to our Father who loves us, and ask Him to multiply them beyond all we could ask or imagine. Let's receive with thankfulness all the blessings He wants to pour out upon our families and our homeschooling days.

what god is saying to my heart

_____

_____

_____

_____

_____

what my heart is saying to god

_____

_____

_____

_____

_____

Dig Deeper: Can you remember a time in your life when God multiplied your efforts? Do you believe He can do the same today?

5

Jesus' power at work in us

Read Ephesians 1:15–23.

M ost of us want to fix everything for everyone.

When my kids were younger, I longed for that elusive feeling that all was right with the world. But often the closest I could get to it was when the kids were safely tucked in their beds, and our house was blissfully quiet (and preferably not a disaster). There was also that rare, fleeting moment when I was able to check off most items on the day's homeschool list.

We live in a sinful, broken world. We dwell here with our imperfect husbands, children, homes, homeschooling plans, churches, communities, and government. Friction occurs when we forget that our hope doesn't actually belong in any of those things.

Even though our here and now can leave a lot to be desired, all that really needs to be right has already been made right. It's easy to forget the most important thing of all: The redeeming blood of Jesus has paid for our sins, so we now have full access to a loving Father. Jesus' resurrection brought redemption, so there is no condemnation for us—ever—for all eternity.

What does that mean for us as we journey on this earth?

> I also pray that you will understand the incredible greatness of God's power for us who believe Him. This is the same mighty power that raised Christ from the dead and seated Him in the place of honor at God's right hand in the heavenly realms.

> — Ephesians 1:19–20

The same power that raised Christ from the dead lives in us! We revel in the hope of eternity and in the power of Jesus.

Moms, we possess the right and privilege of having the powerful, loving, sovereign God walk with us through any circumstance, no matter how daunting, scary, frustrating, overwhelming, or discouraging that circumstance may be. He lovingly disciples us as we look to Him and seek Him with all our hearts.

His desire is to reveal Himself to us continually as we place all our hope in Him.

So be strong and courageous,
all you who put your hope in the Lord!

— Psalm 31:24

what god is saying to my heart

_____

_____

_____

_____

_____

what my heart is saying to god

_____

_____

_____

_____

_____

Dig Deeper: Is your hope fully in God today? Can you see where He is working and the ways He is revealing Himself?

6

god's wisdom or man's?

Read 1 Corinthians 1:18–31.

Although education is important, our society tends to elevate it to an unhealthy place. It has become an idol in many households.

God has a lot to say about worshiping other gods. Throughout the Old Testament, idol worship was the constant downfall of His people. Time and time again, the Israelites turned their backs on God and chose the gods of the culture around them.

When we stop and think about it, we could list several "gods" found in our culture, but as homeschooling moms, the one that plagues us the most is probably the god of education.

While doing what we believe is best for our kids, most of us feel constant pressure and wonder if we'll be able to pull this homeschooling thing off. Why do we think that? Most likely, it's because we've been sent a clear message from the world that we simply aren't good enough—we don't have what it takes.

For thousands of years, children's education happened mostly at home. We've been raised to believe that education is something only certain people can do correctly, but that's not true. In fact, it's irresponsible and reckless.

If you're like me, probably one of the biggest reasons you are homeschooling is that you want your children to own their faith. The world tells us this is foolishness, or at the very least, it tries to distract us with other elements of education. This can make us feel "less than" because we aren't making those elements more important than discipling our children.

I'd like you to reread today's Scripture passage with the things I just mentioned in mind. Notice what God says about the "intelligent" and the "philosophers, the scholars, and the world's brilliant debaters."

As believers, we don't work according to the same economy as the world. We are united with Christ, who is wisdom itself. Our perspective is essentially polar opposite to the world's, so of course our kids' education will look different as well.

God's heart is loving toward us, and He has a very good plan for our children—and for us. We are called to seek His ways above human wisdom, and in that process He will meet our every need.

what god is saying to my heart

_____

_____

_____

_____

_____

what my heart is saying to god

_____

_____

_____

_____

_____

Dig Deeper: Are you listening to the Lord's voice when it comes to your homeschooling, what your days should look like, and how He wants you to interact with your children?

7

my ways or his?

Read Isaiah 50:7–10.

I n today's Scripture reading, Isaiah portrayed an ideal image of Israel. Even though Israel failed to live up to that image, Isaiah's example was realized in Jesus. It is an example God wants us to follow. This side of Heaven, none of us will be able to do it perfectly, but Jesus has us covered where we lack, and we can be confident in our ultimate victory.

We are here to please God, not the voices that condemn and accuse us. That is why it is imperative we pause, reflect, and take time to listen to the Lord's voice in every area of our lives, including our homeschooling.

Even if everyone else is doing something, or the professionals "highly suggest" we do something, we do not have to follow the patterns laid out by the world.

We need to bring our ideas, plans, and challenges before the Lord, knowing He is the One who determines our steps (Proverbs 16:9). In other words, we can (and should) make plans, but we continually need to yield those plans to God and ask for wisdom along the way.

I love the imagery of Isaiah 50:10:

> Who among you fears the Lord and obeys His servant?
> If you are walking in darkness, without a ray of light,
> trust in the Lord and rely on your God.

How many times in our lives and in our homeschooling journey have we felt like we were "walking in darkness, without a ray of light"? That is precisely when we can trust and rely on God.

Isaiah finished the chapter by describing the contrast of trust: living independently and using our own "wisdom" instead of relying on God:

> But watch out, you who live in your own light
> and warm yourselves by your own fires.
> This is the reward you will receive from Me:
> You will soon fall down in great torment.
>
> — Isaiah 50:11

Have you ever felt tormented by your own unreasonable expectations? I sure have! And that's when we can be pretty certain we have stopped relying on Him and started trying to figure things out on our own.

what god is saying to my heart

_____

_____

_____

_____

_____

what my heart is saying to god

_____

_____

_____

_____

_____

Dig Deeper: Are there areas in your life—specifically in your homeschooling—where you feel tormented? In which areas are you relying on God and seeing His faithfulness?

8

the heart of homeschooling

Read Isaiah 44:9-23.

As we begin to catch a better glimpse of the wisdom God reveals in His Word, it becomes painfully obvious that His wisdom looks very different than the "wisdom" of the world. He even calls worldly wisdom "foolishness."

In today's Scripture passage, Isaiah went into detail about how ridiculous it is to worship idols. Verse after verse he described how the craftsman created an idol with the same wood he used to warm himself and bake his bread on. It's easy to see how absurd the man's actions are.

But if we're not careful, we can find ourselves doing something similar with our children's education.

For example, our educational system tells us that our children are not intelligent if they don't pass a standardized test. Every child is given an identical test, though in countless ways one child is not like another. If we rely on this test alone, our children can be categorized, labeled, and quite possibly sent a direction that will do them more harm than good.

This kind of testing doesn't work, yet many homeschooling parents put their hope in that test. They use it as a yardstick to measure their "success" in homeschooling.

I realize we may need our kids to take this test in order to abide by the laws in our states, but I'm talking about an issue of the heart. Are we compromising what God is leading us to do in our homeschooling journey, so we don't feel like "failures" when those test results come in?

Read Isaiah 44:20 again. It's the conclusion to the long description of the idol worshiper:

> The poor, deluded fool feeds on ashes.
> He trusts something that can't help him at all.
> Yet he cannot bring himself to ask,
> "Is this idol that I'm holding in my hand a lie?"

We need to ask ourselves—and God—if what we are holding on to so tightly is a lie. God redeemed us from the lies that weigh us down, which means we can change if we want to.

Isaiah continued:

> "Pay attention, O Jacob, for you are My servant, O Israel. I, the Lord, made you, and I will not forget you. I have swept away your sins like a cloud. I have scattered your offenses like the morning mist. Oh, return to Me, for I have paid the price to set you free."
>
> Sing, O heavens, for the Lord has done this wondrous thing. Shout for joy, O depths of the earth! Break into song, O mountains and forests and every tree! For the Lord has redeemed Jacob and is glorified in Israel.

what god is saying to my heart

_____

_____

_____

_____

_____

what my heart is saying to god

_____

_____

_____

_____

_____

Dig Deeper: Are there any "idols" you need to give up when it comes to homeschooling? Ask God to give you wisdom to know how to "abide by the law" but not lose His heart for your homeschooling days.

9

redeemer of messes

Read Isaiah 45:18–25.

D o you ever feel like God is hiding from you? Are you overwhelmed just at the thought of trying to find Him and hear His voice?

The enemy would love to convince us that God is difficult to find, because that would discourage us from even taking the first step. Not only that, but it would leave a "residue" in our hearts that tells us God is unloving and uncommitted to helping us, to being our God, and to loving us in the ways we need.

> For the Lord is God, and He created the heavens and earth and put everything in place. He made the world to be lived in, not to be a place of empty chaos.
>
> "I am the Lord," He says, "and there is no other. I publicly proclaim bold promises. I do not whisper obscurities in some dark corner. I would not have told the people of Israel to seek Me if I could not be found. I, the Lord, speak only what is true and declare only what is right."
>
> — Isaiah 45:18–19

I remember the day I realized I was always trying to clean up my "messes" before I came to God. What He really wanted was to meet me in the mess and bring redemption. By trying to clean up first, I was sidestepping His grace and attempting to make myself worthy. This seemed to land me in a place of "empty chaos," like Isaiah talked about.

Don't let the enemy convince you that you have to live in "empty chaos." God declares that He is the Lord and there is no other. He is not quiet about proclaiming His promises, nor does He "whisper obscurities from some dark corner." He wouldn't tell us to seek Him if He could not be found.

God loves to answer our prayers. He is our Redeemer, and He takes great pleasure in redeeming the messes in our lives. He brings light in the midst of darkness, clarity in the midst of confusion, peace in the midst of chaos, joy in the midst of grief.

what god is saying to my heart

_____

_____

_____

_____

_____

what my heart is saying to god

_____

_____

_____

_____

_____

Dig Deeper: Are you remembering to invite God into every part of your day—even the messy parts? Have you seen His presence make a difference?

don't go back to egypt

Read Isaiah 30:1–5, 31:1–3, and 48:17–20.

When you're in trouble or feeling overwhelmed, who is the first person you turn to?

In today's Scripture passage, Isaiah confronted Israel for making plans that went directly against God's. Instead of consulting Him, they ran to Egypt for help. This was like a slap in the face to God.

Wasn't God the One who led His people *out* of Egypt? They used to be slaves in that land, held captive and forced to labor for Pharaoh. There was no freedom for them in that place, but somehow they still felt the need to turn back to Egypt for protection when they were attacked.

As we read through the Old Testament, we can see how Egypt represents the world's system and the Israelites represent believers in Jesus. The cross and resurrection allowed us to be grafted into God's family and become His people. He rescued us out of slavery to sin and led us out of "Egypt" into freedom. He redeemed us and made us His own, and right now He is leading us to the Promised Land.

When a powerful enemy attacked Israel, it was frightening and overwhelming for sure—but who did they turn to for help? They formed alliances with the world instead of with the God who rescued them from slavery. In short, they chose to depend on human resources for their protection rather than God.

How many times do we do the same thing? We experience a new physical symptom, and we immediately Google it. We have a disagreement with our husbands, so we call a friend to "vent and get counsel." We feel inadequate in our homeschooling, so we buy new curriculum.

It isn't necessarily wrong to do any of these things, but are we going to the Lord *first* or last or not at all? Are we willing to wait on Him?

Moms, we need to hit the pause button and ask ourselves if we are depending on man's wisdom or God's. We need to remember whom we serve:

This is what the Lord says—your Redeemer, the Holy One of Israel:

> "I am the Lord your God, who teaches you what is good for you and leads you along the paths you should follow. Oh, that you had listened to My commands! Then you would have had peace flowing like a gentle river and righteousness rolling over you like waves in the sea. Your descendants would have been like the sands along the seashore—too many to count! There would have been no need for your destruction, or for cutting off your family name."
>
> Yet even now, be free from your captivity! Leave Babylon and the Babylonians. Sing out this message! Shout it to the ends of the earth! The Lord has redeemed His servants, the people of Israel.
>
> — Isaiah 48:17–20

God has redeemed our lives from slavery. We don't have to go back to Egypt for help, but we can wait on the Lord instead, walking in the freedom He has given us.

> So the Lord must wait for you to come to Him so He can show you His love and compassion. For the Lord is a faithful God. Blessed are those who wait for His help.
>
> — Isaiah 30:18

what god is saying to my heart

_____

_____

_____

_____

_____

what my heart is saying to god

_____

_____

_____

_____

_____

Dig Deeper: Are there areas in your parenting or homeschooling where you may be depending too much on the world? Could God be calling you to let go and trust the wisdom He is giving you?

11

dealing with limitations

Read Isaiah 45:8–12.

D o you ever wonder if you have what it takes to raise your kids to adulthood, much less homeschool them?

It can be so much easier to see where we fall short than to acknowledge our strengths and giftings. But what does God think when we focus on our failures? As our Father and Creator, what is His response when we place our shortcomings under a microscope? Or what about when we let fear get a grip on us because we've been examining our faults?

Reread today's Scripture passage, thinking about the limitations and boundaries you see in your homeschooling.

Is it possible these places where we feel inadequate might actually be limitations God has intentionally allowed? He is the potter, and we are the clay—as are our children. Are we yielding to the mold He wants to use in our lives?

The real question is not if we have shortcomings but how we will view them and what we will do with them.

Lord, You alone are my portion and my cup;
You make my lot secure.
The boundary lines have fallen for me in pleasant places;
surely I have a delightful inheritance.

— Psalm 16:5–6 (NIV)

In this passage from Psalms, do you hear David's clear prayer of dependency on God? "You *alone* are my portion and my cup. *You* make my lot secure." If we had no faults, no weaknesses, no limitations, why in the world would we seek Him?

When we begin to trust God, embrace the boundaries He has on our lives, and respect His right as our Creator to place those boundaries, we find ourselves in a place of peace. Homeschooling from a place of peace makes all the difference in the world.

When we feel unsure about our boundaries, which will inevitably happen, we can think about what David had to say about them:

> I will bless the Lord who guides me;
> even at night my heart instructs me.
> I know the Lord is always with me.
> I will not be shaken, for He is right beside me.

— Psalm 16:7–8

All of us have dealt with concerns about our children and homeschooling that kept us awake at night. I love how David painted a picture of being awake at night, too—but during this time, he was getting counsel and instruction from the Lord.

Instead of lying awake worrying, we can keep our eyes on God and be confident that because He is right beside us, we will not be shaken.

what god is saying to my heart

_____

_____

_____

_____

_____

what my heart is saying to god

_____

_____

_____

_____

_____

Dig Deeper: Are you laying down the details of your family life and trusting God to take care of them? How about your homeschooling? God promises to give you wisdom.

working from a place of rest

Read Luke 10:38–42.

If you're a mom, you're busy. That's just the way it is. The to-do list seems endless and exhausting, and though we often complain about it, most of us don't do anything to change our frantic lifestyles. Why is that?

Some of us feel we have no choice. For thousands of generations, a nurturing nature has driven every mother to do what seemed impossible for the sake of her children. I know I often feel a sense of worth in being needed.

God created us to have these strong nurturing tendencies, but just like anything, when we allow them to hold a position higher than Jesus on the throne of our hearts, it doesn't go well. Something needs to change.

We were created to worship. We are constantly worshiping, and because God made us to worship Him alone, anytime we start to lift up something or someone above Him, we will experience a negative ripple effect.

I am, admittedly, a Martha. I can so relate to her distraction over the details of dinner—the practicalities of life. Seeing to the details is one way I show others love, but at a certain point, I have to ask myself, "Am I really loving, or am I feeding my own sense of worth? And has that sense of worth become an idol in my heart?"

When Jesus responded to Martha's plea for help, He was actually responding to the state of her heart. Her words exposed her worry and hurriedness. She clearly believed that doing something good *for* Jesus took precedence over listening to something good *from* Him.

"Martha, Martha," the Lord answered, "you are worried and upset about many things, but few things are needed—or indeed only one. Mary has chosen what is better, and it will not be taken away from her."

— Luke 10:41–42

We don't have to make the mistake of trying to establish our identity through our work. Instead, we can remember that our identity is shaped and strengthened from a place of rest in God, and then it is *expressed* in our work.

what god is saying to my heart

_____

_____

_____

_____

_____

what my heart is saying to god

_____

_____

_____

_____

_____

Dig Deeper: Do you find it easy to lay down your agenda and good works at the feet of Jesus and just be with Him? When you do this, you put yourself in a position of being able to hear the good He has for you.

13
the only opinion that matters

Read Psalm 37:1–9.

Many times over the years, my husband and I have encountered people who thought the way we were raising or homeschooling our kids was wrong—or at least inferior to what they had in mind.

If God is going to tell anyone how to raise or homeschool your children, it won't be your neighbors, parents, in-laws, out-laws, or friends—it will be you.

As parents, we bear the full responsibility for our children, so it makes sense that God would speak to us when it comes to their well-being. I'm not saying He won't use other people to help us along the way, but we need to be careful that we aren't letting anyone else's opinions change the course we believe God has for our families.

I remember praying about this after an extended family member criticized our parenting. With certain people, you can just smile and nod and move on, but the relationships that matter to us the most can be the ones that wreak the most havoc. We care about these relationships, but sometimes our focus on them can become detrimental. If we aren't careful, we can start to let the opinions of the people we care about carry more weight than the convictions God has placed on our hearts.

No matter how wonderful the person is or has been to us, no opinion should be held above God's direction in our lives. This is a situation where the enemy can get a foothold. At this point, it's not about the person anymore, but it becomes spiritual warfare. We are dealing with an actual enemy.

Reread today's passage with this "enemy" in mind. Focus on verses 5 and 6:

> Commit everything you do to the Lord. Trust Him, and He will help you. He will make your innocence radiate like the dawn, And the justice of your cause will shine like the noonday sun.

When I was struggling to deal with someone else's opinion, the Lord shed light on Psalm 37:1–9 for me. He lovingly reassured me that He had our best interest in mind. He wanted me to move forward in faith, believing that someday others would see the fruit of our obedience to what He was telling us to do. And even if they didn't, we didn't need to fuss about it.

Don't you love the goodness and faithfulness of God? We don't have to concern ourselves with voices that are overwhelming. We simply need to hear from Him.

what god is saying to my heart

_____

_____

_____

_____

_____

what my heart is saying to god

_____

_____

_____

_____

_____

Dig Deeper: Are there areas in your homeschooling life where you know you've heard from the Lord, but now you are doubting His direction because of someone else's opinion? Ask God to give you the courage to walk in obedience to Him.

14

cross centered

Read Isaiah 53:4–11.

S in isn't a fun topic. As homeschooling moms, we are with our kids most of the time, which frequently gives us the opportunity to watch sin play out right before our eyes. Our kids fight. They resist us. They don't do what they're supposed to do, no matter how many charts we create or threats we make.

Then there's us. Painfully aware of our faults and shortcomings, we can become overwhelmed at the thought of having to navigate our kids' sin issues along with our own.

My kids will attest that I have done my share of manipulating, yelling, crying, and throwing all-out hissy fits. It was ugly and certainly not what I envisioned all those years ago before I had children. After these episodes, my heart could hardly bear to think about the nauseating display of sin I just exhibited in front of my children. There were even times I didn't think redemption was possible. I was convinced I had blown it and probably ruined my kids for life.

Reread Isaiah 53:4–11.

But God. But Jesus. But the cross.

Oh, Moms, *this* is when some of the most amazing things can happen! Not because we threw a fit, but because God made a way. He knew we couldn't be perfect, flawless women, so He sent Jesus to His death to pay for our sin—including the hissy fits. When Jesus rose from the dead, He conquered sin and brought redemption to imperfect homeschooling moms everywhere.

When we take these opportunities to bring ourselves and our children back to the cross, when we repent and ask for forgiveness from both God and our children, we communicate how incredibly real our faith is. We show our kids they don't have to be perfect. They can simply be yielded and cross centered.

what god is saying to my heart

_____

_____

_____

_____

_____

what my heart is saying to god

_____

_____

_____

_____

_____

Dig Deeper: Do you feel that your home is cross centered? Are relationships made right through apologies and forgiveness? When sin occurs, do you allow these times to be opportunities to redirect yourself and your kids back to the cross?

wholehearted trust

Read Proverbs 3:1–6.

When I turned ten years old, my grandma gave me a new Bible. She had written out Proverbs 3:5–6 inside the cover in her beautiful cursive handwriting, and every time I opened the Bible, I saw the verses she had written. I read them so often that I eventually memorized them.

Her little note inside my Bible seems like a small gesture, but looking back, I can see the profound impact it had on my life. Why did it have such an impact? I'm not sure, but I wonder if it was because my grandma took the time to give me a taste of the good things that are in God's Word. I love that as moms, we have so many opportunities to give our kids that same taste of goodness.

Read Proverbs 3:1–2 again.

God reminds us not just to hear His direction and correction but to make them an integral part of our lives and walk them out.

God is faithful to shepherd us, just as we shepherd our children. As our Father, He sets the pattern and shows us what it looks like to be a good, loving parent. Sometimes that means correction; other times it means direction.

When we don't understand our circumstances, our husbands, our children, or our friends, we find ourselves trying to gain some sort of insight. We want answers and we'd really like them now, and when they feel out of reach, we often panic and start making decisions out of fear. But we don't have to go down that road.

Trust in the Lord with all your heart; do not depend on your own understanding. Seek His will in all you do, and He will show you which path to take.

— Proverbs 3:5–6

God has a full understanding of every part of our lives. He has perfect perspective, but for me, the best part of all is that He is both sovereign *and* good. He has power over the things we don't, so we can trust Him with every single thing that concerns us. We don't have to try to figure it all out. God doesn't want us to burden ourselves with the things that are simply too much for us.

Instead, He gives us the freedom to trust Him with everything. We can tell Him the things that burden us and seek His face, and He will be faithful to show us what to do next.

what god is saying to my heart

_____

_____

_____

_____

what my heart is saying to god

_____

_____

_____

_____

Dig Deeper: Are you carrying more than you need to today? Are you struggling beneath burdens God wants to carry for you? Take a few minutes to put them into His care.

power over fear

Read Proverbs 3:5-8.

As a young mom, I struggled with the fear of death. It wasn't that I feared where I would spend eternity—I feared that our children would grow up without a mother. They were so innocent and vulnerable, and I was sure that if I died, their future would be bleak at best.

This angst resulted in a personalized version of hypochondria. Every time my body did something new or unusual, fear would grip me and I couldn't seem to stop obsessing. Anytime I felt like I was losing the battle, I would talk with my husband. He was sensible and matter-of-fact, and in my head I knew he was right. But my mom heart was still terrified.

Maybe it isn't over the same things, but have you ever been in that place where no amount of common sense and logic can talk you down from the ledge? Moms, at that point you can be sure your struggle is spiritual warfare.

We are engaged in a battle every single day. The enemy prowls like a lion, seeking whom he may devour. As moms, you hold a powerful position and he knows it. The enemy wants to take you down.

The good news is that as we arm ourselves with God's Word and stand firm, we can send the enemy off skulking like a wounded puppy.

When I realized I wasn't powerless, I asked God to show me how to deal with this crazy fear of mine. Specifically, I asked for something from His Word that could help anchor me. He directed me to Proverbs 3:5-8. Every time I felt fear gripping me, I would pray and stand on verses 7–8 (NIV):

> Do not be wise in your own eyes; fear the Lord and shun
> evil. This will bring health to your body and nourishment
> to your bones.

There are so many voices out there telling us how to eat, drink, exercise, and take care of our bodies. It's confusing and overwhelming and can quickly lead to despair. But God gives us hope through His Word and by His Spirit. We don't have to figure everything out—we just need to seek Him, to slow down our frantic hearts and simply acknowledge Him as Lord above all else. That will bring health to our bodies and nourishment to our bones. He will tell us the next thing we need to know.

what god is saying to my heart

_____

_____

_____

_____

_____

what my heart is saying to god

_____

_____

_____

_____

_____

Dig Deeper: Which areas of your life are you desperately trying to figure out? Will you bring those to Him and leave them in His care?

he is good

Read Psalm 145:13–21.

Whenever I feel overwhelmed with life and motherhood, or when I'm questioning God or deeply grieving, the Psalms are the place where I run. These passages provide a rich testimony of pure faith, yet we can clearly see the authors' humanity as they give us a window into their struggling souls. They share the questions that often accompany deep pain and distress, but they don't leave us there. Everything circles back around to the goodness and faithfulness of God.

It is a comfort to know that God always keeps His promises and is gracious in all He does.

Psalm 145:15–16 gives a beautiful word picture of turning our eyes toward God in hope, and He faithfully fills us with good things. He quenches our deep hunger and thirst, and He gives us what this world cannot offer.

As moms, it's crucial that we understand He truly is the Giver of all good things. No amount of education, knowledge, no material things, earthly relationships, well-behaved children, successful children, public acknowledgement, or anything else can truly bring us the peace we long for, because we were not made for those things.

We were made for relationship with God, to worship Him alone.

Verses 17–18 tell us that He is righteous in all He does. He is filled with kindness, and He is close to *all* who call on Him in truth. It's tempting to question His goodness when we are suffering or distressed, yet His goodness is the very truth we need to stand on as we call out to Him. That is what it means to call on Him "in truth."

When we choose to fear God—to reverence, respect, acknowledge Him—for who He really is above anyone or anything else, He hears our deepest desires and meets them. This is not about a formula—this is about relationship. It's a love exchange between the Creator and His creation, and it is beautiful.

what god is saying to my heart

_____

_____

_____

_____

_____

what my heart is saying to god

I'm feeling very lonely as a sahm. I'm scared my kids wont have friends because I dont even have any.

Dig Deeper: Do you have this kind of relationship with God? Is it easy to question His goodness, or have you experienced it on a deep level? Where in your life could you begin to stand on the truth of His goodness?

freedom from people pleasing

Read Isaiah 51:12–16.

What do you do when a friend, relative, or stranger hassles you about the decisions you've made for your children? Every mom, homeschooling or not, knows exactly what I'm talking about.

From how we feed, clothe, and discipline our kids to school choices and whether or not our kids play sports—I'm not sure why people feel the need to share their opinions, but it can be both exhausting and irritating.

The truth is that each and every one of those decisions is ours to make, and the ramifications of those choices are ours to bear. The weight of parenting our children falls squarely on our shoulders. That thought alone can bring freedom from worrying about what others think. I learned pretty quickly just to smile politely and nod and then go on doing what I thought was best for my kids.

I think many people are well intentioned in their comments and honestly believe they are being helpful, but there are some who simply won't let up. Often those people happen to be related to us or are relationships we can't completely ignore. Those are the ones who make me run to God's Word and ask Him to show me what is true. I want to know what His thoughts are concerning these struggles. I need perspective—His perspective.

As you read today's passage again, be thinking about those who give you the most grief concerning how you parent your kids. Don't you love the vantage point of the Word of God?

"I, yes I, am the one who comforts you. So why are you afraid of mere humans, who wither like the grass and disappear? Yet you have forgotten the Lord, your Creator, the one who stretched out the sky like a canopy and laid the foundations of the earth. Will you remain in constant dread of human oppressors? Will you continue to fear the anger of your enemies?"

God is saying here that we don't have to fear or dread the opinions of others. We are free from that weight. We are a redeemed people who belong to Him, so we don't have to live under that kind of oppression. It's our privilege to choose something else, to choose freedom from other people's opinions.

The dictionary describes freedom as "liberation from slavery or restraint or from the power of another."[1] Jesus has redeemed us from the power of bondage that people pleasing can create.

We are ultimately responsible to our Creator for the choices we make. Sometimes the things other people say cause us to doubt what we are doing, and sometimes God can use other people's questions to give us direction.

However, the best thing we can do is lay all of it out before the Lord and ask Him for wisdom. We can ask Him to show us if there is anything we need to change or do differently, and if He doesn't clearly reveal something, we have the freedom to let it go.

---

1   *Merriam-Webster.com,* s.v. "freedom," accessed December 15, 2017, https://www.merriam-webster.com/dictionary/freedom

what god is saying to my heart

_____

_____

_____

_____

_____

what my heart is saying to god

_____

_____

_____

_____

_____

Dig Deeper: Are there areas in your parenting or homeschooling where you feel the scrutiny of others? Have you taken these areas before the Lord and asked Him for clarity?

wait patiently for him

Read Genesis 2:4–17.

We were never, ever made to live independently of God. Information is at our fingertips all day, every day. Our smartphones, computers, televisions, and other devices feed us an overwhelming amount of information. If we want to know something, we Google it or message someone.

Information can be a blessing, but it's most certainly *not* a blessing if it comes at the cost of depending on God.

After God finished creating the earth and all living things, He laid out boundaries for Adam and Eve. They were simple and straightforward:

> The Lord God placed the man in the Garden of Eden to tend and watch over it. But the Lord God warned him, "You may freely eat the fruit of every tree in the garden— except the tree of the knowledge of good and evil. If you eat its fruit, you are sure to die."

I find the names of the trees intriguing. The tree of life represented God's presence and provision, and the one who ate of it would have eternal life. Eating from the tree of the knowledge of good and evil would open man's eyes to knowledge that would most certainly burden him. It represented a human grasp for autonomy and wisdom that belong to God alone.

We were made for utter and complete dependence on God. Yet the world constantly tells us we need to be independent, autonomous, self-reliant, and choose our own destiny.

Jesus showed us a different way. He Himself was totally dependent on the Father. "I can do nothing on My own. I judge as God tells me. Therefore, My judgment is just, because I carry out the will of the one who sent Me, not My own will" (John 5:30).

God's economy often works in a completely different way than the world's, but His economy is where we are called to live! Therefore, we can safely and confidently take the time to wait on Him for His direction, without panicking or feeling hurried.

Wait patiently for the Lord.
Be brave and courageous.
Yes, wait patiently for the Lord.

— Psalm 27:14

what god is saying to my heart

_____

_____

_____

_____

_____

what my heart is saying to god

_____

_____

_____

_____

_____

Dig Deeper: In which areas of your life do you need to find rest today? Can you find a way to slow down and let your heart be at peace, welcoming the presence and provision God has for you?

mom care

Read Genesis 3:1–7.

I tend to be a bottom-line kind of gal, so when I read today's passage, I see some clear takeaways that are definitely worth noting and keeping in mind on a daily basis.

God clearly laid out the boundaries for Adam and Eve, so they knew what to do if they didn't want to die (Genesis 2:15–17).

We don't know how long Adam and Eve were in the garden before Satan tempted them, but eventually he showed up. The Bible describes him as "shrewd," which can mean smart, intelligent, sharp witted, perceptive, etc. So we can assume his timing was impeccable.

The enemy times his temptations for when we are at our weakest points. When we are overwhelmed, grieving, suffering, or ill, those are optimal times to tempt us to sin, which is why it is imperative we take the time to care for ourselves as moms. We need rest, good nutrition, fresh air, some physical activity, and a little time to ourselves and with God. If we park ourselves on the ragged edge, we will be a constant target for the enemy.

Seeing to our needs isn't about being self-indulgent—it's about positioning ourselves so the enemy doesn't get a foothold in our lives or families. As moms, we are the "hub" of the family. If we fall apart, our families become vulnerable.

The first thing the serpent did was cause Eve to doubt what God actually said. His question was posed in a way that immediately cast a shadow over God's words. It is imperative that we know what God's Word says and we firmly stand on it.

Eve's response minimized all God had given her and her husband. She explained they could eat from *any* tree…except one. It seems to me she was already doubting the goodness of God.

She then went on to soften the certainty of death, which shows a blatant disregard for God's justice, holiness, and hatred for sin. It's crucial we keep who God really is in the forefront of our minds. As we battle the enemy, we take up the shield of faith and the sword of the Spirit, which is the Word of God.

If you are taking some time each day to be in the Word, it makes a huge difference. You don't have to spend a copious amount of time—but enough time to truly remember who He is.

The enemy honed right in on Eve's doubt (verse 4) and confirmed it with a bold-faced lie: "You won't die!"

He put the final nail in the coffin by declaring that God didn't have Adam and Eve's best interest in mind. He was withholding something that rightfully belonged to them. Eve completely fell for it.

These days, we deal with many of the same temptations Eve did. Think about the temptations you have the hardest time resisting. Are they tied to unbelief concerning who God says He is or what His Word says is true? I'm so thankful for His Word and the Holy Spirit as they work in harmony to remind us of the truth that God really is good and, because of that, we can trust Him fully.

what god is saying to my heart

_____

_____

_____

_____

_____

what my heart is saying to god

_____

_____

_____

_____

_____

Dig Deeper: Are you struggling today to believe God's goodness? Take some time right now to remember who He is and recall the ways He has and is caring for you.

building altars

Read Joshua 4:1–7.

Every now and then, our older kids will mention a story from my childhood and the younger ones will say, "What?! I've never heard that one!" It's almost like I've stolen something from them or intentionally excluded them. But what actually happened is that once I told the story, I never thought to repeat it to the ones who probably weren't old enough to understand or maybe weren't even in existence. That is one of the many (sometimes humorous) challenges that can occur in a large family.

In numerous places in the Old Testament, God's people built a memorial to help them remember a defining time in their lives. Usually it was a time when God met them in a very real and powerful way. The altar was a place they could visit over and over again to remind themselves of God's faithfulness.

As humans, we are fickle. We forget—often and quickly. But it's the remembering that breathes fresh life into our faith. When we can slow our hearts down, close our eyes, and think about what we felt when God met us at the place of our deepest need, we begin to sense something rising up within us that moves us toward trusting Him again for our current needs.

Our children need to hear us talk about these defining times we had with God. When we share our stories, our children begin to catch a vision for what faith really looks like.

I love that God not only cares about us, the parents, but also about our children. Through today's passage and many others, He shows us how important it is that we intentionally pass our faith to them. This can happen as we tell stories from the past and pull our kids into conversations about how God is meeting us in our present circumstances.

When we invite our kids into this process, they begin to see they are part of something bigger than themselves. They begin to experience God.

what god is saying to my heart

_____

_____

_____

_____

_____

what my heart is saying to god

_____

_____

_____

_____

_____

Dig Deeper: Think of some of the defining times in your life when God showed up in a big way. Have you told your kids about these experiences?

22

loneliness

Read John 15:15–27.

I think one of the most surprising and difficult aspects of motherhood is loneliness. We can be surrounded by people and still feel isolated.

Motherhood often requires that we pour ourselves out and be constantly accessible, and I think this level of sacrifice might be one of the main reasons moms often feel lonely.

The truth is that feelings of loneliness are rooted less in the number of relationships we have and more in the quality of those relationships.

In today's passage Jesus had one of His last conversations with His disciples before He left them. He reminded them of who they were and that He would send the Advocate (the Holy Spirit) to continue to communicate the truths of God. The Advocate would maintain Jesus' presence in this world, duplicating and sustaining His work.

As we read this passage, we realize the truth: Jesus will *never* leave us, not for one second.

So why do we feel lonely? It could have something to do with the *quality* of our relationships—our relationship with God and quite possibly our relationships with others. When was the last time we slowed our hearts down to contemplate the health of our relationships and to pray over our loved ones? The health of our relationship with God directly affects our relationships with others.

Read verses 26 and 27 again. Jesus assures us that not only will God be with us, but the presence of the Holy Spirit is a gift, one that will give us peace of mind and heart. Do we actually have that peace? Are we enjoying the benefits of knowing God and hearing from Him?

The word *advocate* here is a Greek word that means "called alongside." It is also used in Greek literature in terms of a legal advocate—someone who speaks in a person's defense and provides legal counsel. It is sometimes translated "counselor" and often is interpreted as "comforter." Unfortunately, modern English tends to suggest an advocate is more like a therapist who assures us everything is going to be okay, but the more accurate meaning is one who strengthens and encourages.

I don't know about you, but when I feel overwhelmed and in need of help, I'd rather have help than comfort any day!

Don't you love that? In a culture that seems to be more interested in comfort, God calls us to walk in peace of mind and heart, and He gives us everything we need to do so. Our calling as wives and moms is not outside the scope of His presence or power. In fact, He wants to show Himself in a very real and mighty way—right where we live.

what god is saying to my heart

_____

_____

_____

_____

what my heart is saying to god

_____

_____

_____

_____

Dig Deeper: Do you have peace? Are you walking in a quality relationship with God? Are you enjoying the benefits of knowing Him and hearing His voice as He strengthens and encourages you? Is there any way you can bring more "quality" into your relationships with your children?

contentment

Read Philippians 4:10–13.

"For I can do everything through Christ, who gives me strength."

My guess is that you have heard this verse countless times. This is one of the most-quoted verses in the Bible.

I grew up going to church and have been a regular Bible reader for many, many years, but just a few years ago, I realized I had never actually taken the time to read this verse in context.

If you missed the context the first time, go back and read the passage again.

The theme here is *contentment*. Paul was saying he'd been in many different situations. His life experiences ranged from having much to having little, but in all circumstances, he'd learned the secret of being content. How was he able to have such peace? Through Christ, who gave him strength.

The word *contentment* here does not mean complacency or stoicism, which involve removing our emotions from a situation. We know this because Paul said in verse 10 that he was praising the Lord when he received a gift from the Philippians.

Paul was talking about an inner sense of rest or peace that comes from being right with God and knowing He is in control of all that happens to us. Because we know who He is, we are more concerned with and captivated by Jesus than we are by anything this world has to offer.

Take some time to ponder this. Are you struggling with disappointment in how God is providing for you?

As women, we long to feel secure, to know we are protected, safe, and provided for. Sometimes we really desire nicer things for ourselves or for our children, and in a culture that revolves around achievement and possessions, it can be easy to lose our way. We find ourselves hesitating to trust God because we've been disappointed. But He tells us in 1 Timothy 6:6–10:

> Yet true godliness with contentment is itself great wealth. After all, we brought nothing with us when we came into the world, and we can't take anything with us when we leave it. So if we have enough food and clothing, let us be content.
>
> But people who long to be rich fall into temptation and are trapped by many foolish and harmful desires that plunge them into ruin and destruction. For the love of money is the root of all kinds of evil. And some people, craving money, have wandered from the true faith and pierced themselves with many sorrows.

Although Paul was clearly referring to materialism, I can't help but wonder if the idea of contentment might apply to other areas as well. How often do we wish we were better at something—so we could be better homeschooling moms? Math is not an area of natural strength for me, but not only did God call us to homeschool our children, but He also gave us several kids who *love* math. I knew in my heart I didn't have the time to try to re-learn and "teach" math to my kids. After praying about it and asking God to give me wisdom, I watched Him provide everything we needed in very unique ways with each child.

God created us. He knows us inside and out. He is a faithful provider, but sometimes His provision doesn't look like what we were hoping for. It's important that we remind ourselves of the truth and don't let the enemy get a foothold. If he can, he will lead us down the road of discontentment, which could also be called distrust. Even when God's provision looks different than we expected, we can have full confidence that it is good and that it is enough.

what god is saying to my heart

_____

_____

_____

_____

what my heart is saying to god

_____

_____

_____

_____

Dig Deeper: Are you holding on to feelings of discontentment? Are you ready to trust that God is providing for you and that He will continue to provide in all areas?

24

shining like stars

Read Philippians 2:12–18 (NIV).

What does it mean to "work out your salvation with fear and trembling"?

We are saved by grace, but in today's passage Paul told believers to do something that doesn't always make sense right at first. How can we be saved by grace *and* work out our salvation with fear and trembling at the same time? Paul wasn't contradicting himself. Instead, he was reminding us that when we received God's gracious salvation, He brought such a massive change to our hearts that it altered the way we do things. We no longer live by the world's standards. As God's power works within us, we move with Him. It is His power that makes us able to do His will and walk in obedience.

Complaining happens *fast*. Whether chatting with people in "real life" or scanning posts on social media, we don't have long to wait before running straight into someone complaining. And right away, others try to join in, adding their own complaints to the mix. As the old saying goes, "Misery loves company." It's almost like some sort of bonding occurs between us when we complain, but that sense of kinship is only a cheap substitute for healthy relationships. Rarely does complaining lead to problem-solving or helpful information. Instead, it seems to progress naturally into arguing. This is especially tempting for us as moms. I often refer to it as "mommy martyrdom."

In today's passage Paul clearly said to do *everything* without complaining or arguing. Everything. Period. I don't know about you, but as a homeschooling mom, I can find myself "venting," and honestly it has never been helpful for me. Yes, it might have successfully guilted my kids or husband into helping me, but could I have asked for help and skipped the complaining? Yes.

Complaining and arguing are a favorite foothold of the enemy, and he can get a lot of mileage out of them. They are a regular battle at our house—and they are surprisingly contagious. Once that freight train gets going, it's really hard to stop it!

Paul gave an interesting reason as to why we need to avoid complaining and arguing:

> . . . so that you may become blameless and pure, "children of God without fault in a warped and crooked generation." Then you will shine among them like stars in the sky as you hold firmly to the word of life.
>
> — Philippians 2:15–16

If we are complaining and arguing, we aren't acting any differently than the world. Why would people be drawn to a salvation that—apparently—has not made us any different than the warped and crooked generation we live in?

There's really only one way to counteract complaining. We have to replace it with gratitude. As Colossians 3:17 (NIV) says, "And whatever you do, whether in word or deed, do it all in the name of the Lord Jesus, giving thanks to God the Father through Him."

what god is saying to my heart

_____

_____

_____

_____

_____

what my heart is saying to god

_____

_____

_____

_____

_____

Dig Deeper: Is there too much complaining going on at your house? How about in your own heart? Science has proven that gratitude can rewire the brain for a more positive (God-honoring) thought life and attitude. Find two or three verses you can write down to help remind you to be thankful, and put them in strategic locations.

if not, he is still good

Read Habakkuk 3:16–19.

Not that long ago, many of us didn't really know all that was going on in the world. The internet brought an unprecedented awareness and with it the burden of knowledge.

In the Garden of Eden, Adam and Eve chose to break God's command and eat of the tree of the knowledge of good and evil. That tree represented man's grasp for autonomy and independence from God. When Adam and Eve fell, all mankind fell, and we continue to live with the results of the fall today.

We are inundated with the knowledge God wanted to spare us from, and now we have to deal with more of it than ever.

As we see the wickedness that takes place all around us, we are forced to answer certain questions: Why does God allow injustice? Why does He tolerate evil? These are hard questions, and many unbelievers claim they are the reason they can't believe God exists or that He is good.

Habakkuk is a tiny book included among the Bible's minor prophets. (They bear that name because they are shorter than other books, not because they are less important.) Habakkuk asked God the same questions we do about what He allows and how He executes judgment. God didn't answer Habakkuk's questions directly. Instead, He gave him a vision of His deity. This was God's way of saying to Habakkuk—and to us—that whether or not we understand His ways, we *can* safely trust Him.

We all have areas in our lives that are hard—things that happened beyond our control, things we feared would happen. We have relationships that seemingly can't be mended and children and husbands who struggle for reasons we don't understand. Some of us grapple with purpose and destiny because we feel inadequate, and yet we can't deny that He's called us.

When our youngest child was twenty months old, he developed acute ITP, which is the shortened name of a condition that mimics early symptoms of leukemia. This same child had open heart surgery at three days old and spent the first two months of his life in the hospital. We almost lost him back then, but God spared his life. Now two years later, we faced the possibility of leukemia. It turned out he did not have cancer, but we didn't know if his condition was a one-time thing (acute) or would recur throughout his life (chronic).

During the waiting period, I thought I might just curl up and die. The fear and stress were overwhelming, and yet God sent people and moments to me when I felt His strong presence at just the right times to sustain me.

When we finally knew that Silas' condition would happen only once, I wrestled hard with God about the whys. The whole event felt pointless and I told Him so. There was nothing I could do but wait to hear from God, and so that was what I did.

Finally I heard Him whisper to me, "Did I keep Silas?"

Yes, He had.

"Did I keep you?"

Yes, He had.

Once my questions were answered, peace flooded over me, and even though His answers weren't what most would call "complete," the Holy Spirit enabled me to embrace them and lay it all to rest.

There are no easy answers to the hardest questions of life, but as believers, we have solid reasons to exercise our faith and trust in our very powerful, very good God.

Even though…

Yet I will rejoice in the Lord! I will be joyful in the God of my salvation! The Sovereign Lord is my strength! He makes me as surefooted as a deer, able to tread upon the heights.

— Habakkuk 3:17–19

what god is saying to my heart

_____

_____

_____

_____

_____

what my heart is saying to god

_____

_____

_____

_____

_____

Dig Deeper: Faith is where we put our gaze. Where is your gaze today?

wisdom for everything

Read James 1:5–8.

After having kids, I've never read any Scripture more than I've read James 1:5–8. It is my go-to passage for wisdom.

If you've been a mom for more than ten minutes, you've felt it—the blaring realization that you really don't know what you're doing. It's one thing to watch other people parent, but when the responsibility of raising and caring for children falls directly on your shoulders, the weight can feel almost unbearable.

We love our kids in ways we never thought possible, but we have this gnawing feeling it may not be enough. We need direction—specific direction. In those moments, I have leaned *hard* into today's passage.

When we run into roadblocks with homeschooling, discipline, relationships, communication, learning styles, financial burdens . . . nothing is off limits when it comes to praying this passage in James.

James encouraged us to ask for what we need, but he also reminded us that God is generous. We aren't asking someone without the means to help us. He owns the cattle on a thousand hills. He created the universe and provided the very specific pieces of our environment to sustain us: just the right ratio of oxygen to carbon dioxide, the perfect amount of gravity to keep us from floating off but not crush us, the sun to warm us but not destroy us, and so much more. He lovingly and generously provided these things. Why do we expect Him to stop there?

James went on to assure us that God won't be upset when we ask. What He does want is for us to put our faith in Him alone. The implied question is whether or not we are divided in our loyalty. James was saying that in order to receive wisdom from God, we must ask for it, fully trusting that every ounce of the wisdom we need will come from Him alone.

Every time I find myself thinking I might not receive the wisdom I need, my anxiety increases dramatically. "A wave of the sea, blown and tossed by the wind." I am doubting that God can handle the enormous burden I'm carrying. I've learned that if I am still in a panic or feel anxious after praying, it is because I'm not really putting my full trust in Him, acknowledging He is both able and willing to make a way. Fear as opposed to trust is driving me.

Here's one of my favorite verses to pray in this kind of situation: "Lord, I do believe, but help me overcome my unbelief." This comes from the story in Mark 9 where a father brought his demon-possessed child to Jesus and asked for healing. He believed, but admittedly, his belief was weak. This happens to me more often than I care to admit, but I love that even in this weak place, God meets me and increases my faith. I simply need to ask.

what god is saying to my heart

_____

_____

_____

_____

_____

what my heart is saying to god

_____

_____

_____

_____

_____

Dig Deeper: Do you have anything specific that continues to make you feel anxious, even after you've prayed about it? What would happen if you asked God to help your unbelief?

no worries

Read Philippians 4:4–8.

Anxiety has become an epidemic in our society, and for moms, the battle seems to multiply exponentially.

What would it be like if you didn't really know how other moms were disciplining, feeding, diapering, or educating their children? On the one hand, knowing these things can be reassuring, but on the other hand, it can really mess with your thinking. Yesterday you might have been perfectly content with your diet, but today you are questioning everything you put in front of your children. Anxiety builds, and with it comes feelings of inadequacy and tension.

In today's passage Paul said not to worry about anything—but we should pray instead. When I'm praying, I'm not worrying, but when I'm worrying, I'm not really praying. Yes, I could shoot up something that *sounds* like a prayer, but is it really prayer if it is not accompanied by faith?

So instead of worrying, we should pray about everything. We can tell God what we need and thank Him for all He has done. There are two important elements in this process:

1. We can be specific in our prayers. We can pour our hearts out to Him, because He wants details. I've found that when I pray specifically, God answers specifically. In most cases, a hurried, frantic heart talking on the fly isn't going to take the time to pray specifically. We have to slow our hearts.

2. We need to be thankful. We need to remember and acknowledge what we have seen God do. This isn't for His benefit—it's for ours. It builds our faith.

As we do these things, we will experience God's peace that exceeds anything we can understand. His peace becomes a protection for our hearts. Then, as a continued safeguard, we practice the discipline of taking our thoughts and fixing them on what is true, honorable, right, pure, lovely, admirable, etc.

Learning how to do this from other moms can be a huge blessing. If it weren't for certain women in my life who did things differently than I did, I never would have made some of the good changes God wanted for our family. At the same time, we need to be sure we are following His lead in those decisions, rather than reacting out of fear.

God loves us beyond anything we could ever imagine. He has good things for us, and His timing is always perfect. He continually sustains the birds of the air and lilies of the field. If He cares so wonderfully for these "insignificant" things, and He considers us to be of higher value, why wouldn't He fully provide for us as well?

I love that God gave us feelings that help warn us when something isn't right. When we feel anxious, those emotions can actually make us aware there is a problem. The key is to bring the problem before Him, listen for His answers, and walk in obedience. That is what it looks like to live from a heart of trust.

what god is saying to my heart

_____

_____

_____

_____

_____

what my heart is saying to god

_____

_____

_____

_____

_____

Dig Deeper: Are you feeling anxious? What specific thing do you need to ask God for? What are you thankful for?

28

looking like fools

Read 1 Corinthians 1:18–31.

As moms, all of us have been plagued by the thought that what we're doing and how we are doing it simply isn't adequate. Maybe it's just me, but I have struggled with this weight off and on for many, many years.

I would look at the simple way we were homeschooling and think to myself, *If someone looked from the outside in, they would surely say I'm not doing enough. I would look utterly foolish to them.*

Did you notice in today's passage how God turns that kind of thinking on its head? He even addresses the people the average person would greatly respect. I think of psychologists, child development specialists, doctors, and educators who have years of training and experience, but maybe they have no relationship with God whatsoever. I believe God can still use them, but His wisdom is so much greater than the wisdom of the world. Even the most brilliant and well-educated (and often well-meaning) professionals can be seriously limited in their understanding, while God's understanding and wisdom have no end. There is no way to measure the greatness of God.

> Instead, God chose things the world considers foolish in order to shame those who think they are wise. And He chose things that are powerless to shame those who are powerful.
>
> — 1 Corinthians 1:27

The world may look at homeschooling moms as "powerless," yet according to this passage, those are the exact ones He will use mightily. This simplicity, which the world's wise and brilliant people sometimes call foolish, is often actually the wisdom of God.

I'll give you an example. Even though I occasionally questioned the simplicity of our homeschooling, God would always somehow reassure me. He would show me that I needed to continue down this path and trust Him for the rest. That can feel like a huge leap of faith, but those leaps never go unnoticed. God sees them because He sees our hearts. It was hard at times, but I chose to be obedient.

The other day, one of our sons who recently graduated told me something that amazed me. He appreciated that we hadn't overloaded them with information and content. Instead, we kept things simple, and he said this left room for questions. He would find himself sitting with a simple statement or two about chemistry, and this would stir up questions in his mind about the whys. He would research the answers, and in the process he learned far more than I could have ever forced him to learn.

This is just one of the many ways God convinced me of the importance of listening to His voice above all—even if it means feeling "foolish" from time to time.

In verse 22 Paul pointed out that the Greeks thought only human wisdom mattered, but they called the simplicity of the cross "foolishness." (As a side note, our school system is based on the Greek method of teaching, so even at its foundation, it is based on human wisdom.) As believing homeschooling moms, we are called to something so much more meaningful as we raise and educate our children. Our lives are cross centered, not world centered. This makes all the difference because our redemption in Jesus changes everything.

If God has called us to homeschool, He will challenge us to think outside the box, but He won't leave us without the wisdom, strength, and grace to walk in obedience to Him.

what god is saying to my heart

_____

_____

_____

_____

_____

what my heart is saying to god

_____

_____

_____

_____

_____

Dig Deeper: What are some ways you feel "foolish"? If you believe God is directing you to do those things, are you willing to look foolish in order to walk in obedience to His plan for your family? Is it possible that looking foolish for the sake of the cross could include raising and educating your kids in a way that seems very different from the world?

finding meaning in the mundane

Read 1 Corinthians 1:18–31.

The other day, I was talking with our married daughter who has two children under the age of three. She was sharing with me how hard it is to continue to do the same, seemingly mundane things every single day and feel like what she is doing is important, that it matters.

My mind immediately went to today's passage because it articulates God's heart so well. When I read it, the "mundane" parts of motherhood fit perfectly. It makes sense that God would take what seems meaningless to the world and use it for His glory:

> Instead, God chose things the world considers foolish in order to shame those who think they are wise. And He chose things that are powerless to shame those who are powerful. God chose things despised by the world, things counted as nothing at all, and used them to bring to nothing what the world considers important. As a result, no one can ever boast in the presence of God.
>
> — 1 Corinthians 1:27–29

God uses the message of the cross to turn human wisdom upside down. As believers, we live with this reality every day. Every diaper changed, every meal made, every toilet cleaned, every book read to the kids, every mess cleaned up, every snuggle given, every conversation we choose to engage in (or some semblance of engagement with the very little ones) absolutely counts as important.

Thinking about life this way requires humility, and when I consider Jesus' ministry and life on this earth, the following passage stands out in my mind. It describes His ultimate example of humility:

> Though He was God, He did not think of equality with God as something to cling to. Instead, He gave up His divine privileges; He took the humble position of a slave and was born as a human being. When He appeared in human form, He humbled Himself in obedience to God and died a criminal's death on a cross. Therefore, God elevated Him to the place of highest honor.
>
> — Philippians 2:6–9

God honors humility. Jesus said in Matthew 23:12, "But those who exalt themselves will be humbled, and those who humble themselves will be exalted." He notices and He blesses an attitude of humility.

Mark 9:33–37 brings closure to all we've read and leaves us with a beautiful picture of motherhood:

> After they arrived at Capernaum and settled in a house, Jesus asked His disciples, "What were you discussing out on the road?" But they didn't answer, because they had been arguing about which of them was the greatest. He sat down, called the twelve disciples over to Him, and said, "Whoever wants to be first must take last place and be the servant of everyone else."
>
> Then He put a little child among them. Taking the child in His arms, He said to them, "Anyone who welcomes a little child like this on My behalf welcomes Me, and anyone who welcomes Me welcomes not only Me but also My Father who sent Me."

what god is saying to my heart

_____

_____

_____

_____

_____

what my heart is saying to god

_____

_____

_____

_____

_____

Dig Deeper: As you do the "menial" tasks of motherhood today, remind yourself that you are not just serving your children—you are serving Jesus. In addition, remember your identity isn't found in what you do but who you are. Do you see yourself as a daughter of the Most High King? Because that's the truth!

redemption in motherhood

Read Isaiah 64:1–9.

I often tell moms that they have the most important job in the world, because they do. I also tell them it's a very powerful role the enemy would love nothing more than to destroy.

When discussing the importance of motherhood, most of us probably think of how influential we are in our children's lives. They start out dependent upon us for everything. Although it can feel overwhelming at times, this season is truly a gift. A part of every woman was made to nurture, so the gratification we feel as we care for our babies is tangible during this time.

But this dependency upon Mom is only temporary. The natural course is that our children become more and more able to take care of themselves. We, in many ways, are waiting for them to grow up, and in the meantime, our hands stay busy.

For the believing mom, much more can occur in motherhood than simply raising children. We can start to become more like Jesus. As we seek Him with our whole hearts, we undergo a deep transformation that carries an eternal impact.

In Isaiah 64:1–4 the prophet declared the greatness of God, His mighty deeds, and how He works on behalf of those who wait for Him. This is our reality: The things we need most will be achieved for us by the labor of God or not at all. He is the Strong One, and just as our young kids are dependent upon us, we are dependent upon Him.

Unfortunately, we often forget this dependency, and in forgetting, we can all too easily give the enemy a foothold in our lives. We can get caught up in trying to be the perfect mother—or, at the very least, not ruin our kids for life.

In this place we have very important decisions to make, because while we are busy fretting over whether or not we are doing everything right, we could be missing the more important battle.

As we try desperately hard to be better moms, it is possible to start destroying ourselves through anxiety, shame, and even idolatry. Especially when I first started mothering, there were many, many things that took up far more space in my heart than they deserved. I was anxious about so much that was really a waste of time. I dealt with feelings of unimportance and shame that cropped up through the challenges I faced.

Our culture is bent on being noticed and feeling important, but we weren't created to receive these things from the world. We were created to find our identity in God, to know who we are in Him. As we discover this identity and embrace it, we begin to live our lives from a place of rest, trust, and peace.

God has something far better than our human attempts, but we need to choose to cooperate with the redemptive work He wants to do through motherhood. All of us bring baggage into this mom role—and God intends to redeem all of it. Everything. His heart toward us is unceasingly good, pure, and perfect. For every step we take toward Him, He more than meets us with His unmatchable warmth and grace.

what god is saying to my heart

_____

_____

_____

_____

_____

what my heart is saying to god

_____

_____

_____

_____

_____

Dig Deeper: Which season of motherhood are you in right now? No matter what is going on in your family, are you trusting God to take care of you and the ones you love? As you wait on Him in faith, consider Isaiah 64:4 and understand how true it is in your life: "For since the world began, no ear has heard and no eye has seen a God like You, who works for those who wait for Him!"

unhurried grace

Read Psalm 27

You're a mom, so every day of your life brings challenges. Some challenges are merely unexpected, but others broadside us like a semi-truck. One thing we can count on is that we will be involved in a spiritual battle. The role we play as wives and moms is a powerful one with the potential to change the world. The more we seek God's heart and walk in obedience to Him, the more the enemy is going to push back. There are times it feels as though we can't overcome, but nothing could be further from the truth.

In Psalm 27 David was clearly feeling this kind of pressure and pushback from his enemies. As he poured out his heart to God, his voice was a mix of confidence and lament, and what bound them together was his longing for God's presence.

All of us hear voices that accuse and condemn us and tell us we are not enough. They can come through our past experiences, social media, relatives, acquaintances, even total strangers, and yet they all originate from the same place—the enemy of our souls. If we can recognize their source, we can wage a more effective war, and our chances of victory increase exponentially.

One of the key elements of victory in any battle is strategy. We need to know our enemy and his tactics, so we can arm ourselves, be prepared, follow orders from our commanding officer, and stay focused.

The enemy of focus is distraction. Our enemy can and will try to distract us, and more often than not, the tool he uses is busyness.

Busyness is not the same thing as diligence. Busyness is defined as "lively, but meaningless activity."[2] Its fruit is a hurried life that causes us to forget

2   (http://www.dictionary.com/browse/busyness)

our sense of God-given purpose. We exchange God's peace for chaos, confusion, and exhaustion. Eventually we come to accept those things as part of our identity, and they make our yoke of service much heavier than it needs to be.

Jesus said in Matthew 11:28–30 (MSG):

> Are you tired? Worn out? Burned out on religion? Come to Me. Get away with Me and you'll recover your life. I'll show you how to take a real rest. Walk with Me and work with Me—watch how I do it. Learn the unforced rhythms of grace. I won't lay anything heavy or ill-fitting on you. Keep company with Me and you'll learn to live freely and lightly.

Jesus wants to walk alongside us as a gentle shepherd, showing us how to walk, work, and rest in "unforced rhythms of grace." The first step toward this kind of peace is taking the time to slow our hearts on a regular basis and walk in relationship with Him.

I know your days are full, caring for your family and other people, and this is a good, good thing—it is a gift from God. However, relationships grow best in unhurried time. It takes courage to slow down and wait on God, but it's in the unhurriedness that we find the fullness of His endless grace.

Wait patiently for the Lord.
Be brave and courageous.
Yes, wait patiently for the Lord.

— Psalm 27:14

what god is saying to my heart

_____

_____

_____

_____

_____

what my heart is saying to god

_____

_____

_____

_____

_____

Dig Deeper: Do you have a strong sense of God-given purpose today? Where is your focus? Do you need to say "no" to certain things so you can walk in "unforced rhythms of grace" with Him?

conclusion

My heartfelt prayer is that this short study of the Word has deepened your understanding of God and you are more acutely aware of what He is saying to you. I hope you will continue to set your heart even more fully upon Him and receive all He has for you. He is a good Father, and He has *good* things for you and your family!

Now to him who is able to do immeasurably more than all we ask or imagine, according to his power that is at work within us, 21 to him be glory in the church and in Christ Jesus throughout all generations, for ever and ever! Amen (Ephesians 3:20,21 NIV).

about the author

Durenda married Darryl in 1989, and she is a mom to eight kids born less than thirteen years apart. She always considered motherhood to be the ultimate career, but she had no idea of the countless ways it would deepen and humble her. Many, many times she found herself unsure and struggling, only to discover God's strength at the end of her rope. She realized she experienced the grace she desperately needed when she took the time to slow her heart and listen for His still, small voice. Her greatest joy is helping moms discover that grace as well—and with it the courage to put their full trust in Him as they learn to hear His voice above all others.

How to find Durenda

DurendaWilson.com
Facebook: facebook.com/durenda.wilson.official
Instagram: @durendaleewilson
Twitter: @DurendaWilson

Made in United States
North Haven, CT
26 April 2023

35927311R00078